TITAN BOOKS

To the loving memory of Snowball I:
If you're in kitty heaven, we hope you're
sitting in the catbird seat.

SIMPSONS COMICS WINGDING Copyright ©1996 & 1997 by
Bongo Entertainment, Inc. All rights reserved.

Published in the UK by Titan Books Ltd., 42-44 Dolben Street,
London SE1 0UP, under licence from Bongo Entertainment, Inc.

FIRST EDITION: JUNE 1997

ISBN 1-85286-806-6
2 4 6 8 10 9 7 5 3 1

Publisher: MATT GROENING
Managing Editor: JASON GRODE
Art Director / Editor: BILL MORRISON
Book Design: MARILYN FRANDSEN
Legal Guardian: SUSAN GRODE

Contributing Artists:
TIM BAVINGTON, JEANNINE CROWELL BLACK,
CHRIS CLEMENTS, LUIS ESCOBAR,
STEPHANIE GLADDEN, TIM HARKINS, NATHAN KANE,
BILL MORRISON, PHIL ORTIZ , STEVE STEERE, JR.

Contributing Writers:
TRACY BERNA, GARY GLASBERG, JIM LINCOLN, BILL MORRISON,
JEFF ROSENTHAL, DAN STUDNEY, SIB VENTRESS

PRINTED IN CANADA

CONTENTS

DON'T CRY FOR ME, JEBEDIAH!

HEADS UP, RADIO-ACTIVE MAN! IT LOOKS LIKE YOU COULD USE A HAND--OR SHOULD I SAY *FIST?!*

BARTMAN! I SURE AM GLAD TO SEE *YOU!* I'M GOING TO NEED ALL THE HELP I CAN GET IN ORDER TO STOP THE REIGN OF TERROR BROUGHT ON BY...

EL BARTO

SCRIPT & PENCILS PG 1-3	LAYOUTS	PENCILS	INKS	LETTERS	COLORS	MISTER MIRACLE
BILL MORRISON	LUIS ESCOBAR	CHRIS CLEMENTS	STEVE STEERE, JR.	JEANNINE CROWELL	NATHAN KANE	MATT GROENING

9

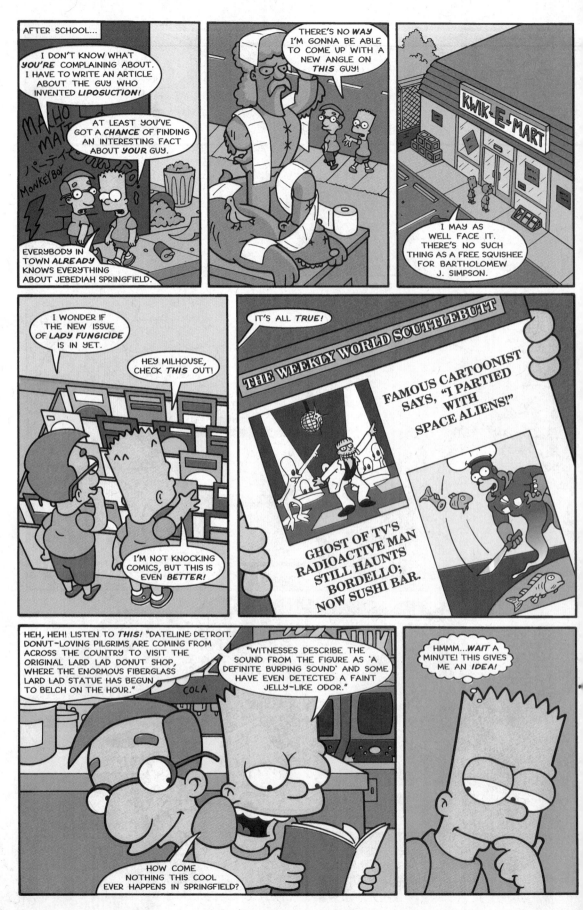

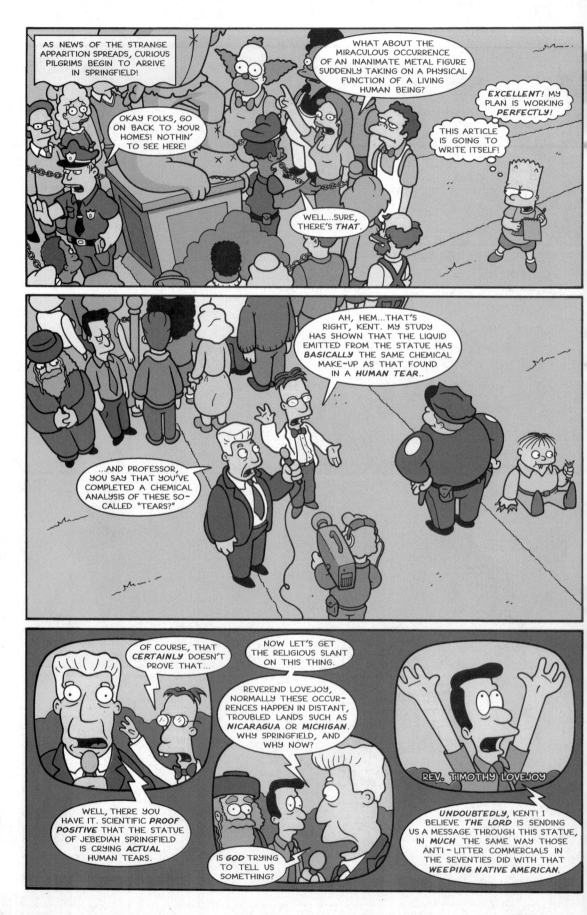

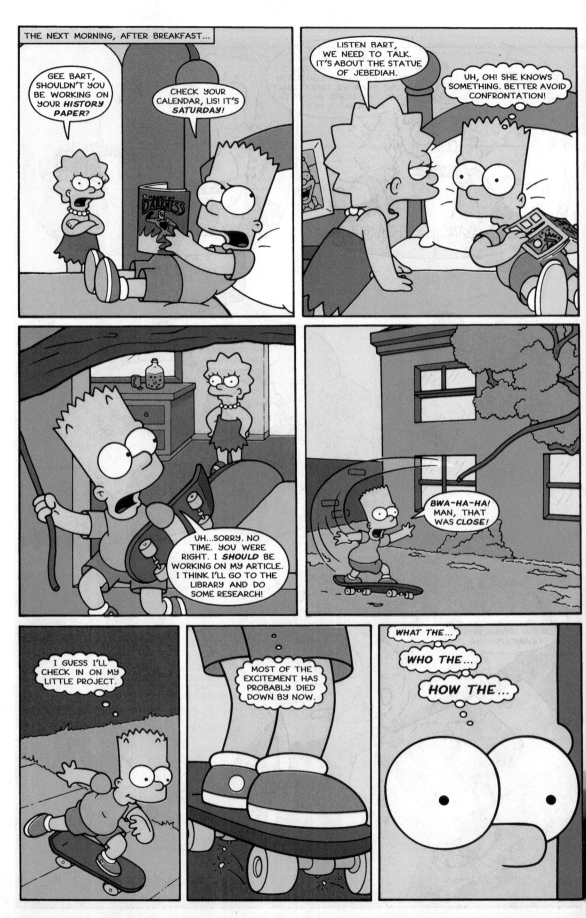

21

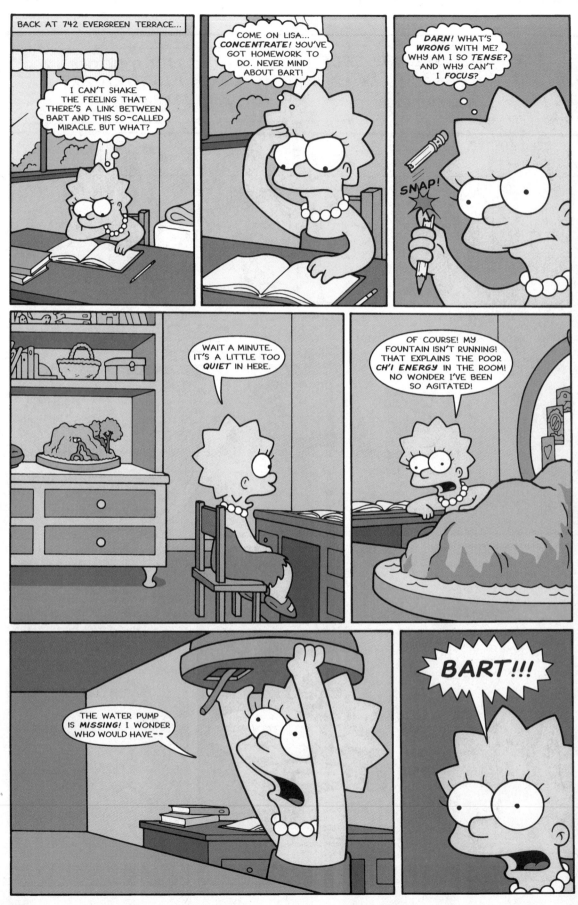

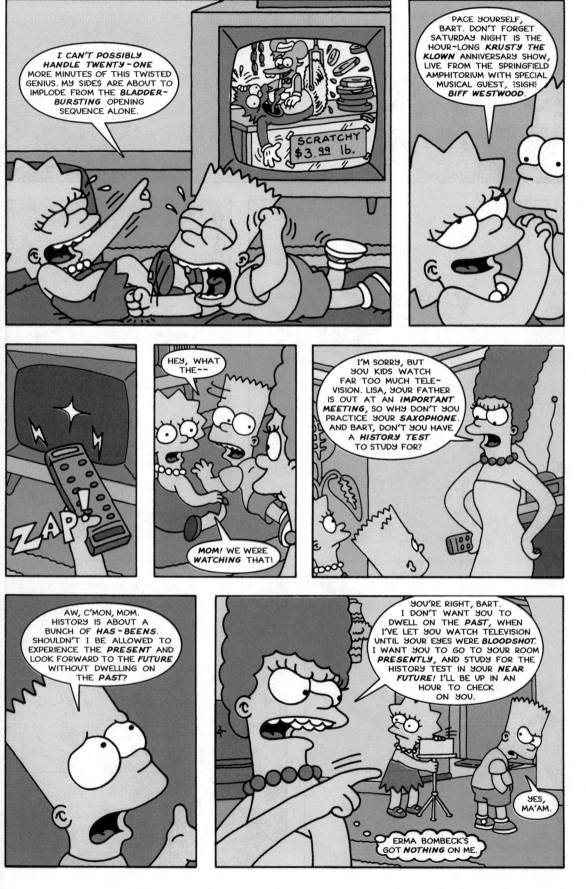

I CAN'T POSSIBLY *HANDLE TWENTY-ONE* MORE MINUTES OF THIS TWISTED GENIUS. MY SIDES ARE ABOUT TO IMPLODE FROM THE *BLADDER-BURSTING* OPENING SEQUENCE ALONE.

SCRATCHY $3.99 lb.

PACE YOURSELF, BART. DON'T FORGET SATURDAY NIGHT IS THE HOUR-LONG *KRUSTY THE KLOWN* ANNIVERSARY SHOW, LIVE FROM THE SPRINGFIELD AMPHITORIUM WITH SPECIAL MUSICAL GUEST, :SIGH: *BIFF WESTWOOD.*

ZAP!

HEY, WHAT THE--

MOM! WE WERE *WATCHING* THAT!

I'M SORRY, BUT YOU KIDS WATCH FAR TOO MUCH TELE-VISION. LISA, YOUR FATHER IS OUT AT AN *IMPORTANT MEETING,* SO WHY DON'T YOU PRACTICE YOUR *SAXOPHONE.* AND BART, DON'T YOU HAVE A *HISTORY TEST* TO STUDY FOR?

AW, C'MON, MOM. HISTORY IS ABOUT A BUNCH OF *HAS-BEENS.* SHOULDN'T I BE ALLOWED TO EXPERIENCE THE *PRESENT* AND LOOK FORWARD TO THE *FUTURE* WITHOUT DWELLING ON THE *PAST?*

YOU'RE RIGHT, BART. I DON'T WANT YOU TO DWELL ON THE *PAST,* WHEN I'VE LET YOU WATCH TELEVISION UNTIL YOUR EYES WERE *BLOODSHOT.* I WANT YOU TO GO TO YOUR ROOM *PRESENTLY,* AND STUDY FOR THE HISTORY TEST IN YOUR *NEAR FUTURE!* I'LL BE UP IN AN HOUR TO CHECK ON YOU.

YES, MA'AM.

ERMA BOMBECK'S GOT *NOTHING* ON ME.

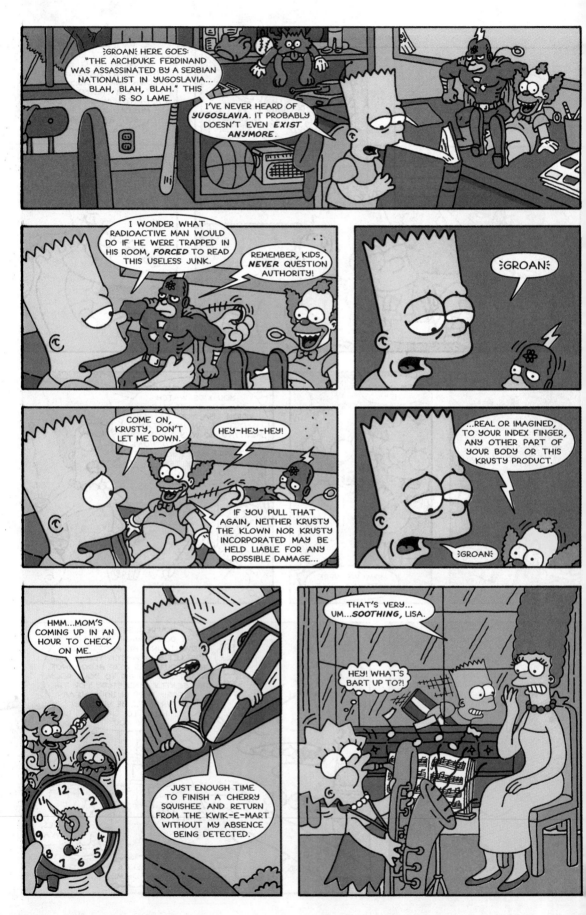

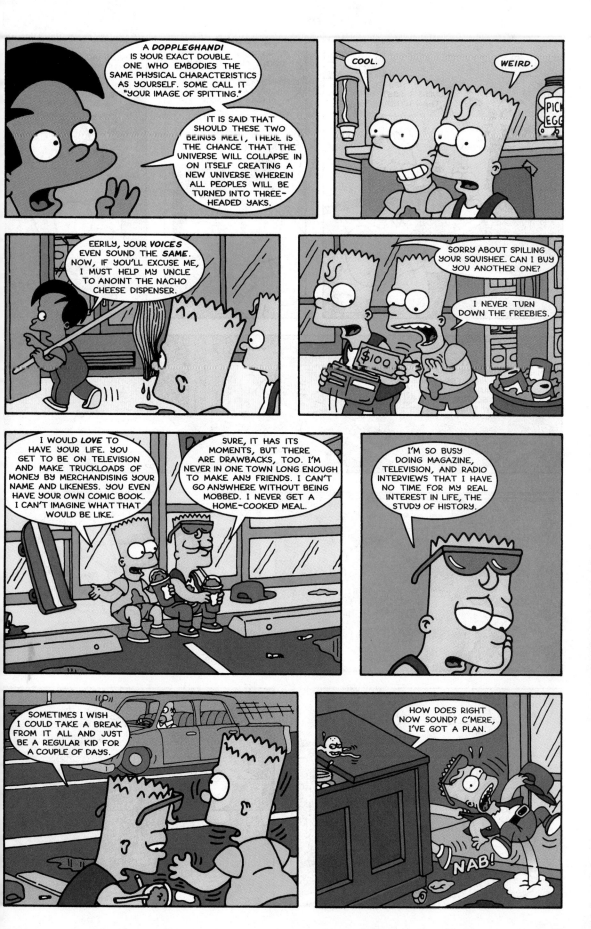

33

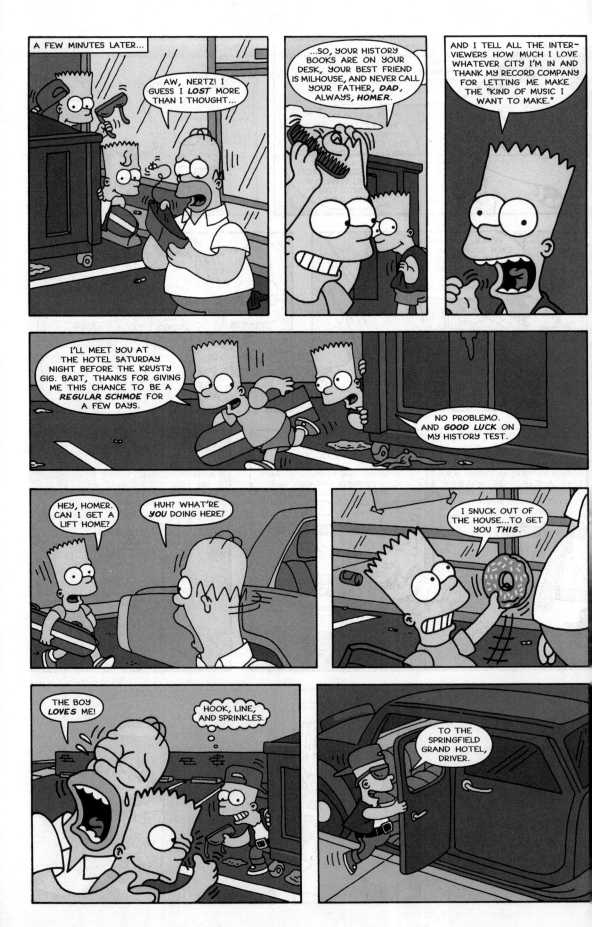

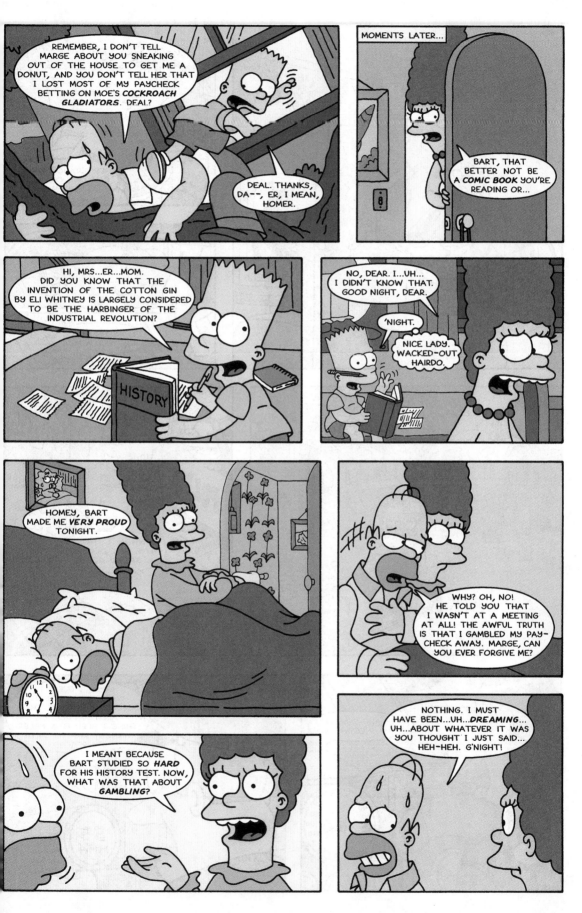

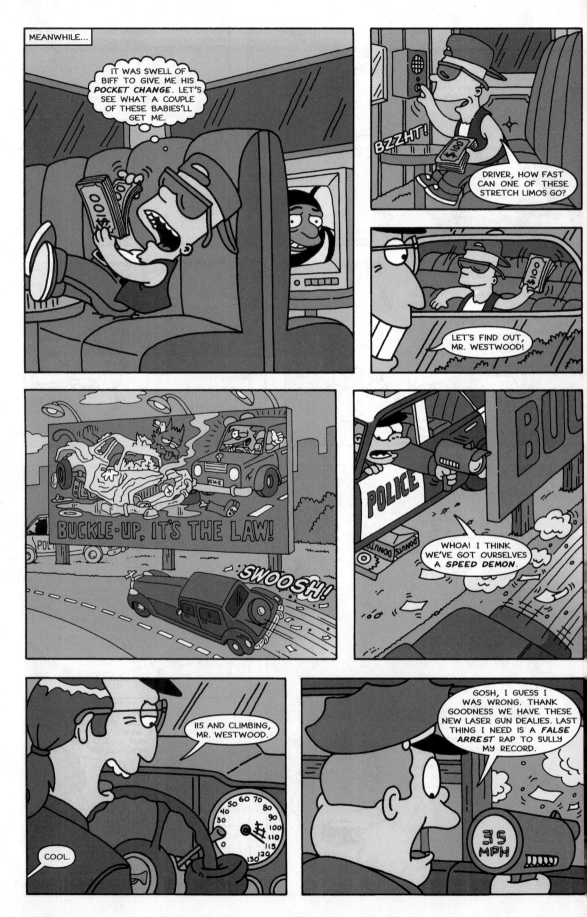

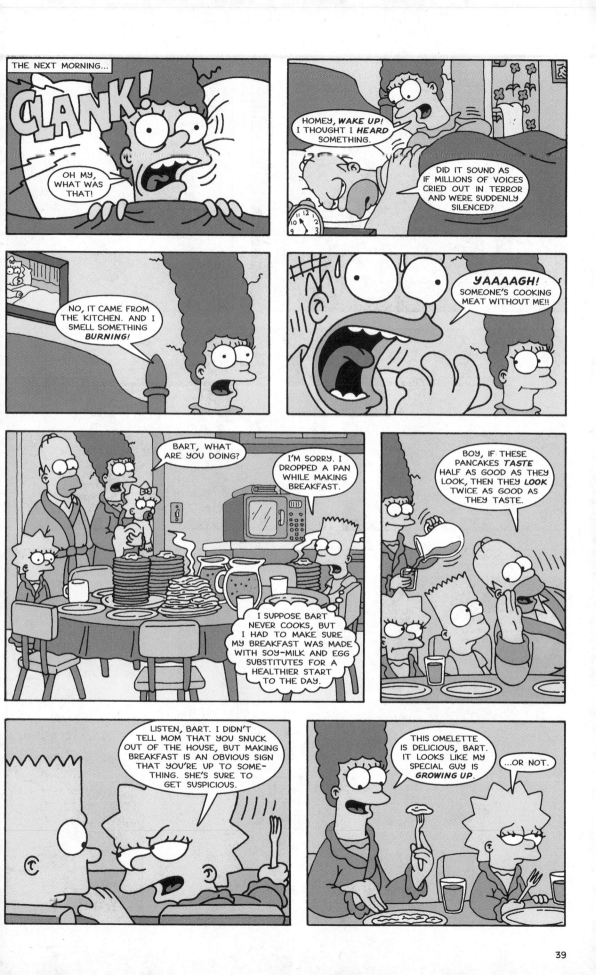

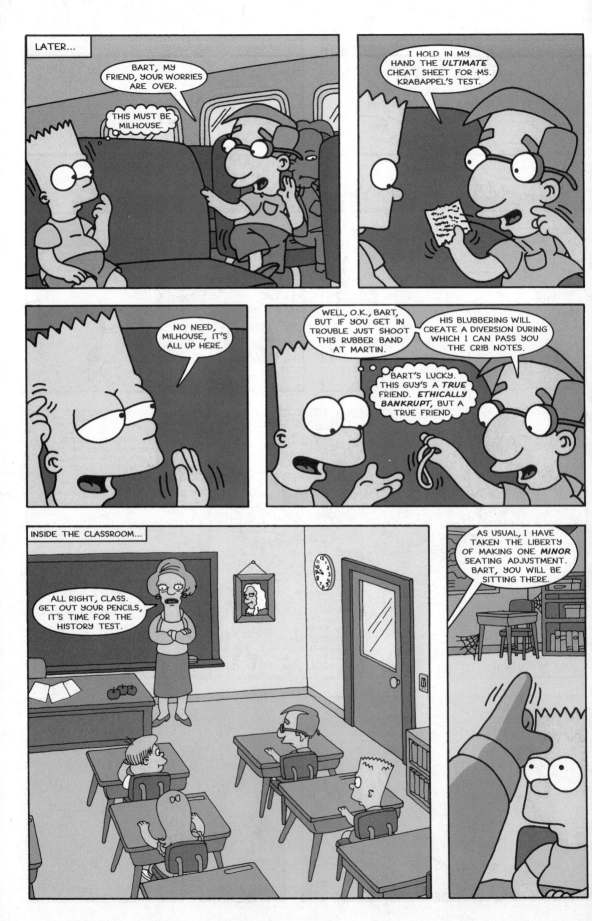

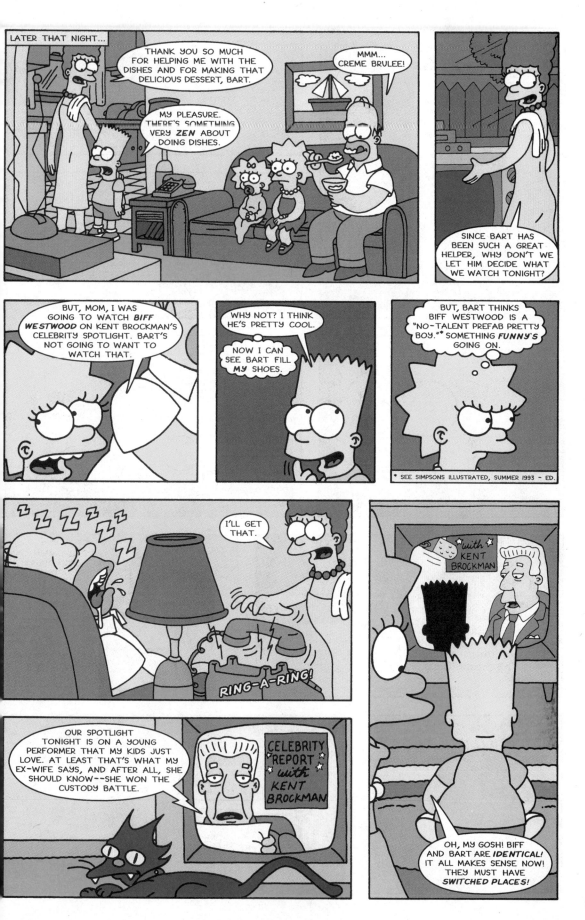

LATER THAT NIGHT...

THANK YOU SO MUCH FOR HELPING ME WITH THE DISHES AND FOR MAKING THAT DELICIOUS DESSERT, BART.

MMM... CREME BRULEE!

MY PLEASURE. THERE'S SOMETHING VERY *ZEN* ABOUT DOING DISHES.

SINCE BART HAS BEEN SUCH A GREAT HELPER, WHY DON'T WE LET HIM DECIDE WHAT WE WATCH TONIGHT?

BUT, MOM, I WAS GOING TO WATCH *BIFF WESTWOOD* ON KENT BROCKMAN'S CELEBRITY SPOTLIGHT. BART'S NOT GOING TO WANT TO WATCH THAT.

WHY NOT? I THINK HE'S PRETTY COOL.

NOW I CAN SEE BART FILL *MY* SHOES.

BUT, BART THINKS BIFF WESTWOOD IS A "NO-TALENT PREFAB PRETTY BOY."* SOMETHING *FUNNY'S* GOING ON.

* SEE SIMPSONS ILLUSTRATED, SUMMER 1993 — ED.

I'LL GET THAT.

RING-A-RING!

with KENT BROCKMAN

OUR SPOTLIGHT TONIGHT IS ON A YOUNG PERFORMER THAT MY KIDS JUST LOVE. AT LEAST THAT'S WHAT MY EX-WIFE SAYS, AND AFTER ALL, SHE SHOULD KNOW--SHE WON THE CUSTODY BATTLE.

CELEBRITY REPORT *with* KENT BROCKMAN

OH, MY GOSH! BIFF AND BART ARE *IDENTICAL!* IT ALL MAKES SENSE NOW! THEY MUST HAVE *SWITCHED PLACES!*

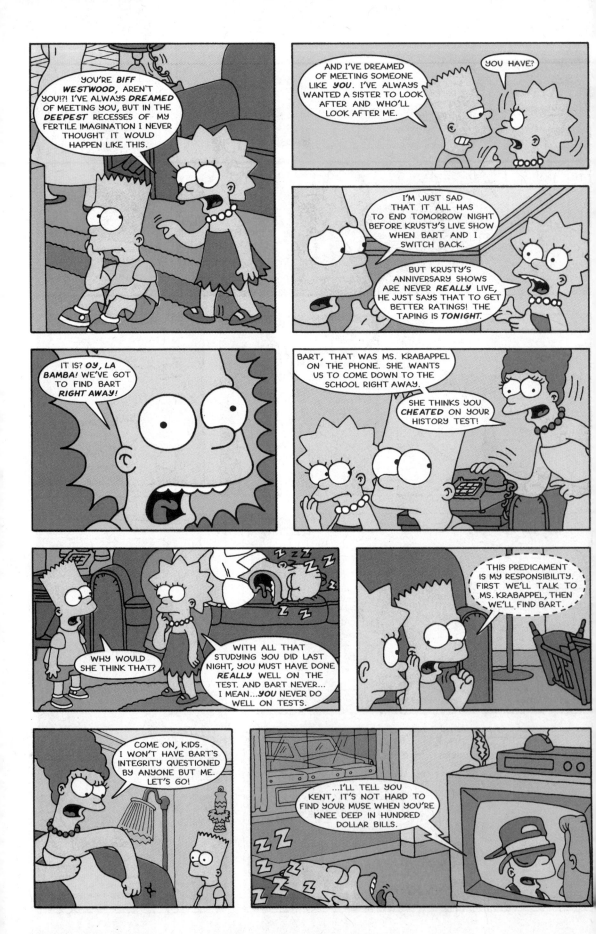

MEANWHILE...

...AND MAKE SURE YOU CATCH MY CAMEO ON THE NEW HIT SERIES, "SPRINGFIELD SHORES."

I PLAY A BLOATED CORPSE THAT WASHES UP ON THE BEACH RIGHT IN THE MIDDLE OF THE COPPERTONE BIKINI NATIONALS!

EVEN FROM BACKSTAGE, I CAN *FEEL* HIS POWER AS AN ENTERTAINER.

★ BIFF ★ WESTWOOD

KRUSTY THE CLOWN

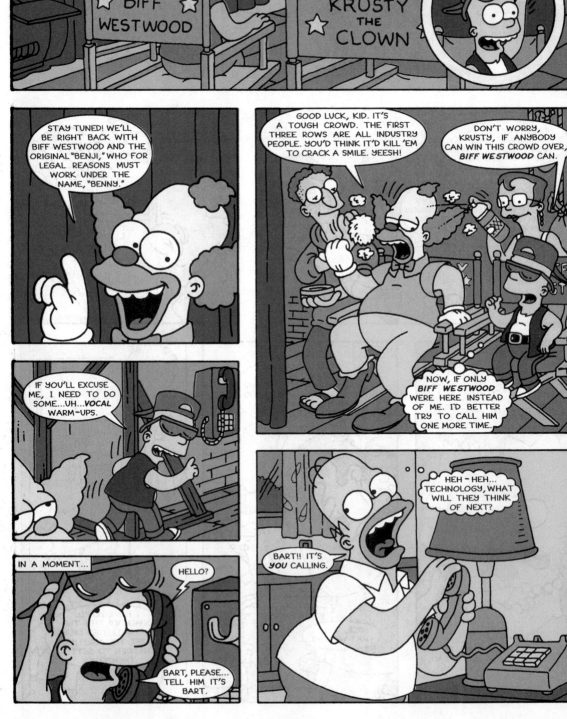

STAY TUNED! WE'LL BE RIGHT BACK WITH BIFF WESTWOOD AND THE ORIGINAL "BENJI," WHO FOR LEGAL REASONS MUST WORK UNDER THE NAME, "BENNY."

GOOD LUCK, KID. IT'S A TOUGH CROWD. THE FIRST THREE ROWS ARE ALL INDUSTRY PEOPLE. YOU'D THINK IT'D KILL 'EM TO CRACK A SMILE. YEESH!

DON'T WORRY, KRUSTY, IF ANYBODY CAN WIN THIS CROWD OVER, *BIFF WESTWOOD* CAN.

IF YOU'LL EXCUSE ME, I NEED TO DO SOME...UH...*VOCAL* WARM-UPS.

NOW, IF ONLY *BIFF WESTWOOD* WERE HERE INSTEAD OF ME. I'D BETTER TRY TO CALL HIM ONE MORE TIME.

HEH—HEH... TECHNOLOGY, WHAT WILL THEY THINK OF NEXT?

BART!! IT'S *YOU* CALLING.

IN A MOMENT...

HELLO?

BART, PLEASE... TELL HIM IT'S BART.

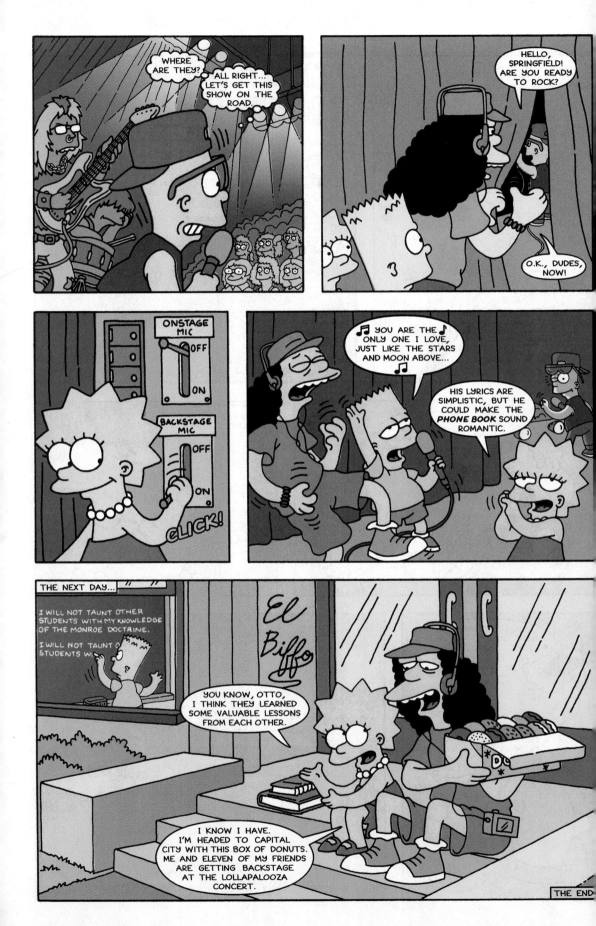

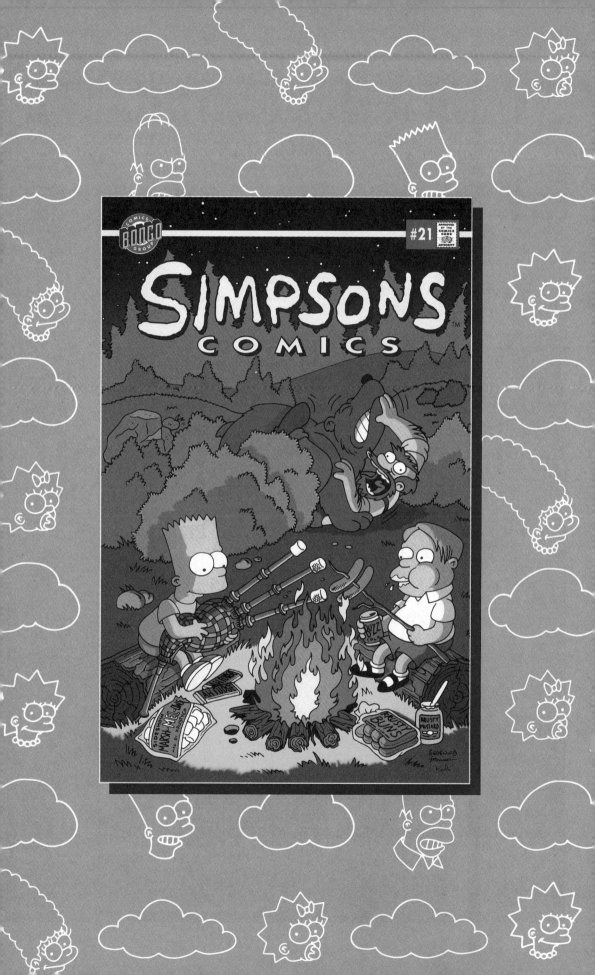

STAND AND DELIVERANCE

THE SCHOOL BOARD PICKED THE *BEST* POSSIBLE TIME TO INSPECT OUR BELOVED SPRINGFIELD ELEMENTARY.

I MUST SAY, I *TOTALLY* AGREE WITH THOSE *NO-NONSENSE BUDGET CUTS* THE BOARD RECOMMENDED.

I CAN ASSURE YOU THAT I'M *PERSONALLY* INVOLVED WITH EVERY CENT THAT IS SPENT HERE!

SCRIPT SIB VENTRESS & TRACY BERNA	**PENCILS** PHIL ORTIZ **INKS** TIM BAVINGTON	**COLORS** & **ART SUPERVISION** NATHAN KANE	**LETTERS** JEANNINE CROWELL **MOUNTAIN MAN** MATT GROENING

INEVITABLY...

¡TEACHER

ICE COLD SODAS

=SIGH=

KRUSTY SODA

KRUSTY SODA

KRUSTY SODA

SOON...

CHALMERS IS RIGHT --MY ADMINISTRATION IS A *SHAM!*

I NEED A WAY TO TEACH THESE KIDS THE VALUE OF *DISCIPLINE*, OF *HONEST WORK*...WITHOUT RAISING THE IRE OF THE P.T.A. OR I'LL BE THE MIDNIGHT TO EIGHT-MAN AT THE *MEGA-MART* BEFORE SPRING BREAK!

I'VE GOT AN IDEA... A *BRILLIANT* IDEA!

...AND A CRAMP. OOOCH.

Glider

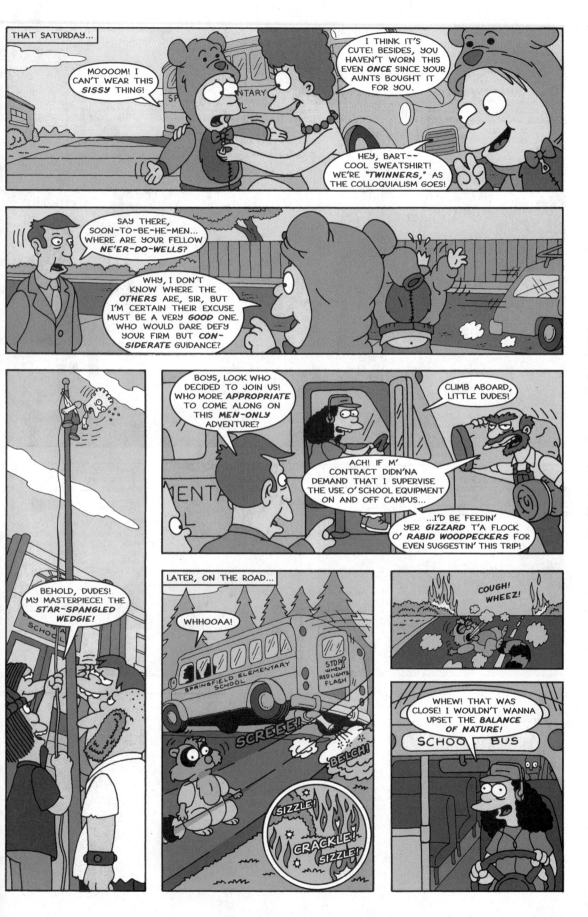

55

YOU KNOW, WHEN WE GET WHERE WE'RE GOING, YOU BOYS HAD BETTER KEEP YOUR EYES PEELED --SOME PRETTY *STRANGE THINGS* CAN COME OUT OF THE WOODS, SOME PRETTY *STRANGE PEOPLE,* TOO... WHICH REMINDS ME OF A STORY. YOU SEE, NOT EVERY SPRINGFIELD ELEMENTARY FIELD TRIP HAS TURNED OUT *HAPPILY.*

THAT'S RIGHT! THE *BALL BEARING FACTORY* STILL HASN'T REOPENED!

HEH! HEH! HEH!

KNOW WHERE YOU STAND GET YOUR BEARINGS! MANAGEMENT

MASTER CONTROL

BALL BEARINGS

OVER-RIDE

WHAT DID THAT KID *DO?*

WE HAVE BEEN FORSAKEN!!!

WELL, THAT EXPLAINS THIS *VOLUMINOUS* PARENTAL RELEASE FORM...

NO SIR, WE HAVEN'T.

HAVE YOU BOYS HEARD THE *HORRIBLE* STORY OF THADDEUS JACKSON?

YEARS AGO, MR. JACKSON WAS A YOUNG, IDEALISTIC TEACHER AT SPRINGFIELD ELEMENTARY...

HE THOUGHT THAT, DESPITE THE *LOW PAY* AND *GOVERN-MENT CUTBACKS,* HE COULD USE KINDNESS, ENERGY AND IMAGINATION TO ACTUALLY MAKE HIS STUDENTS *CARE* ABOUT LEARNING.

SOUNDS LIKE *FRESH MEAT.*

HE TOOK PITY ON SOME *YOUNG MISCREANTS* LIKE YOU, SIMPSON, AND DECIDED THAT SOME *EXTRA ATTENTION* MIGHT BE JUST THE THING THEY NEEDED. SO HE ENDEAVORED TO TAKE THEM ON A *FIELD TRIP* MUCH LIKE OURS, TO CATALOG THE LOCAL FLORA AND FAUNA...

SPRINGFIELD ELEMENTARY SCHOOL

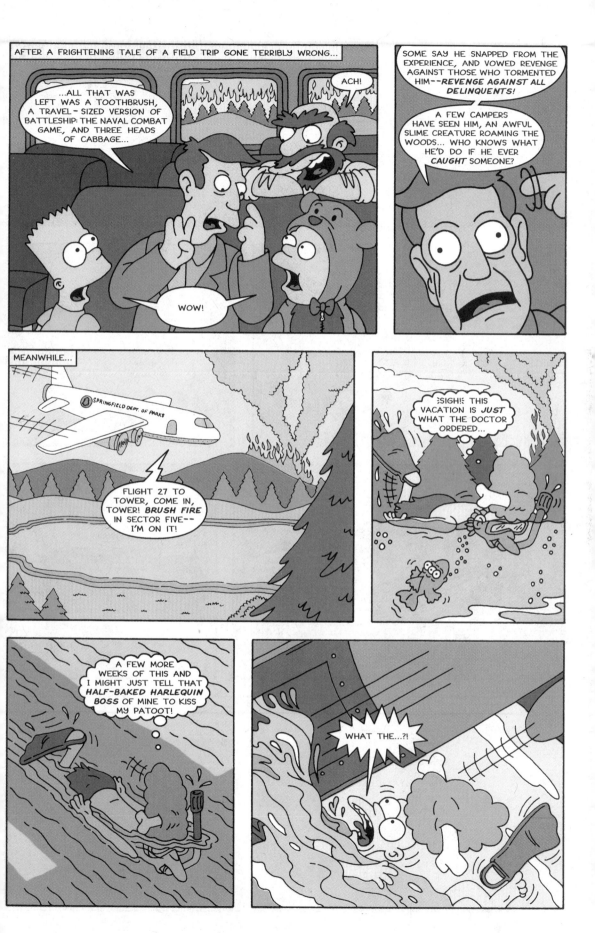

59

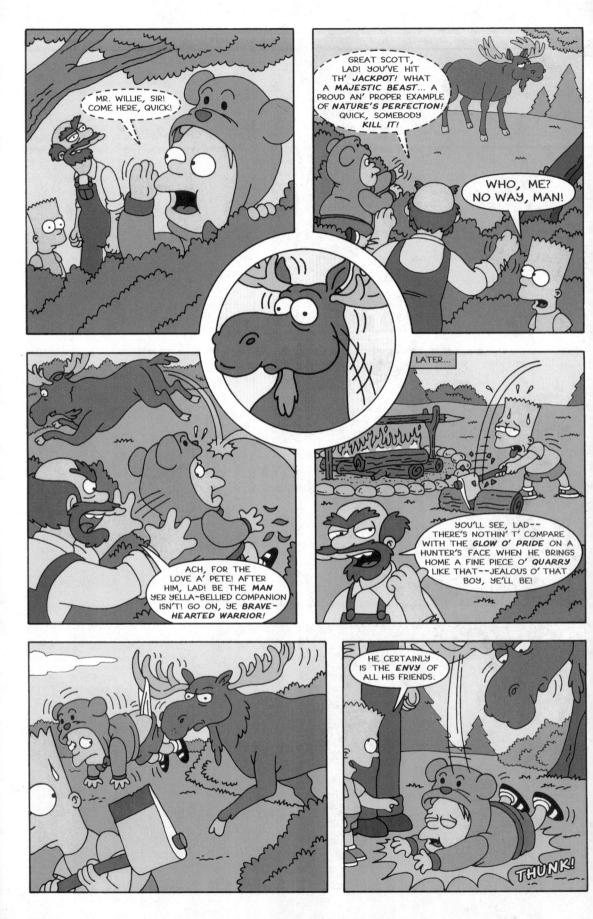

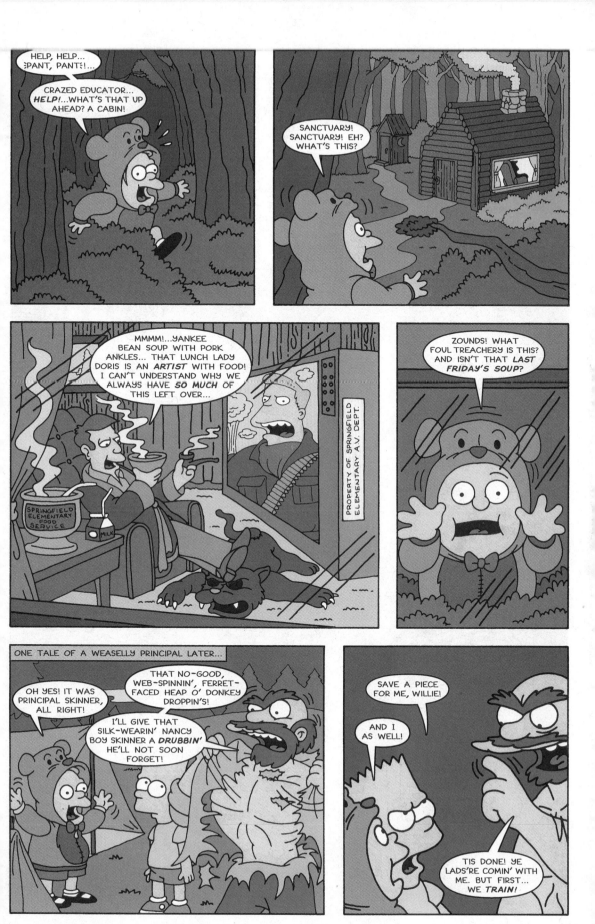

THE TIME DRAWS NIGH, ME WEE *FEARLESS GLADIATORS*. ARE YE READY?

AYE, WILLIE!

YOU TWO GO; THERE'S NO HOPE FOR ME. THIS TRAINING HAS *BROKEN* MY *BODY*, MY *SPIRIT*...AND WORST OF ALL, MY *PEN!* THIS SHIRT IS LINEN-- IT'LL NEVER COME OUT.

ACH! THEN IT'S JUST THE *TWO* OF US! LET'S NA *WASTE* ANOTHER MINUTE. WE'RE OFF!

SHORTLY...

THERE'S THE SCURVY *TRAITOR* NOW...HE'LL NEVER KNOW WHAT *HIT* 'IM!

NOW PUT YER SHIRT BACK ON-- YER GIVIN' ME THE CREEPS.

I'LL TAKE TH' ROOF WATCH, LAD; Y'KNOW WHAT TO DO 'ROUND BACK!

HMM..."WHITE BLOOD CELLS: THE BODY'S FOOT SOLDIERS" OR "SPONTANEOUS CELL DIVISION IN AMOEBAS"...AM I IN THE MOOD FOR SOMETHING *INSPIRING* OR *RACY*...?

65

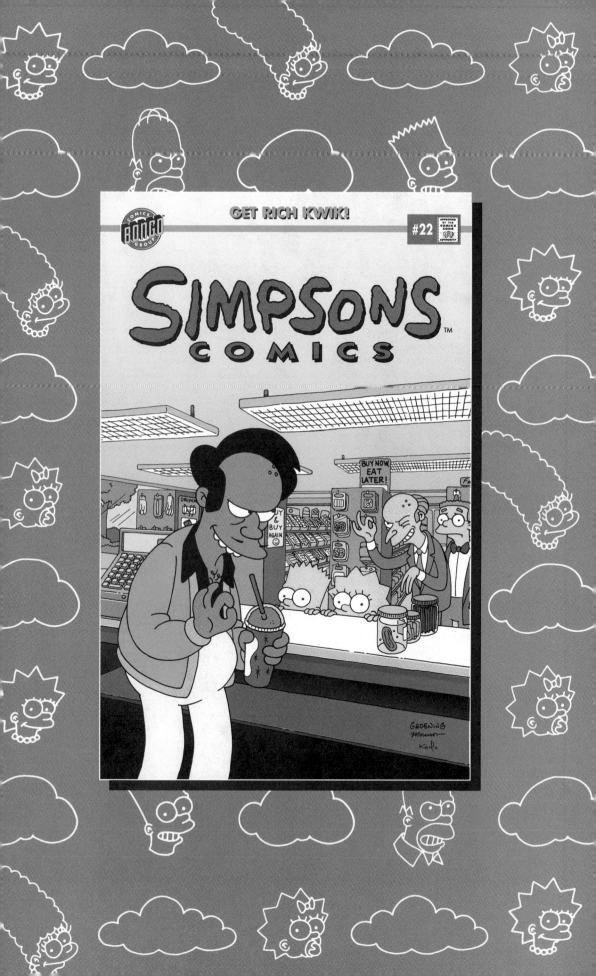

EH! WHO KNOWS! THE QUESTION IS, WILL MARKETING SPECIALISTS *CHANGE* THE KWIK-E FORMAT TO CATER TO TODAY'S *YOUNGER, COFFEE HOUSE CLIENTELE?*

DO I LOOK LIKE A CAST MEMBER OF A POPULAR *TWENTY-SOMETHING SITCOM* TO YOU?

AS WE BOTH KNOW, I DO NOT. THUS, I FEAR FOR MY CONTINUED EMPLOYMENT.

POOF!

THIS *BAT* HAS SEEN SO MANY CUSTOMERS COME AND GO. WHO CAN I *COUNT* ON FOR *PATRONAGE,* IF AND WHEN THAT WHICH IS GOING BEGINS TO GET TOUGH?

SQUISH

2 FO

RADIOACTIVE SQUADRON TO BASE--WE'VE INFILTRATED THE REFUELING STATION. PREPARE TO *LAUNCH!*

I'M *SO HUNGRY* I COULD EAT A KWIK-E-DOG WITHOUT *HOLDING MY NOSE!*

PLEASE! SHOW SOME RESPECT FOR MY MEAT AND MEAT BY-PRODUCTS!!

IGNITION! RADIOACTIVE POD REACHING WARP SPEED!

OOPS. SORRY APU. DIDN'T MEAN TO *CHEESE YOU OFF!*

HEH, HEH! UH, *GOOD ONE,* BART!

SPROING!

SPLAT!

NACHOS

I WILL ALLOW IT TO GO THIS TIME, YOUNG SIMPSON. I WILL MERELY *MASK* THE TASTE AND COLOR OF THE *MOLTEN PLASTIC* WITH A FEW ADDITIONAL CHUNKS OF RED HOT CHILI PEPPER!

NOW WHAT KIND OF SQUISHEE CAN I DO YOU FOR TODAY?

MEANWHILE, IN THE OFFICE OF CHARLES MONTGOMERY BURNS...

ARE YOU WATCHING THIS, SMITHERS? WHO IS THAT INDIAN GENTLEMAN BEHIND THE COUNTER?

THE CHEROKEE OR NAVAJO, SIR?

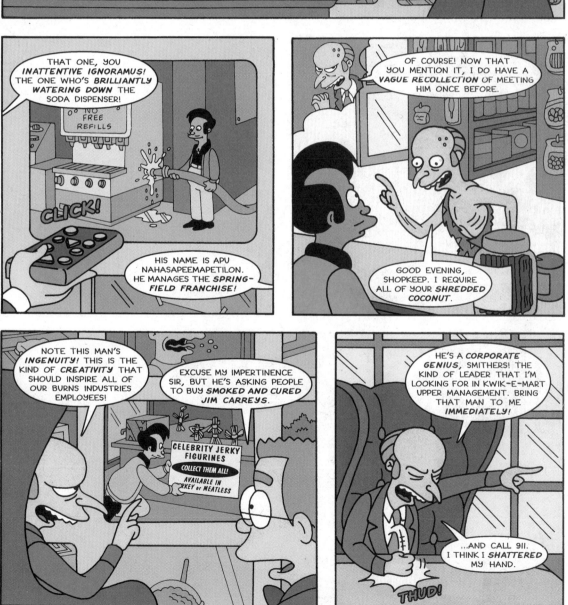

THAT ONE, YOU INATTENTIVE IGNORAMUS! THE ONE WHO'S BRILLIANTLY WATERING DOWN THE SODA DISPENSER!

NO FREE REFILLS

CLICK!

HIS NAME IS APU NAHASAPEEMAPETILON. HE MANAGES THE SPRINGFIELD FRANCHISE!

OF COURSE! NOW THAT YOU MENTION IT, I DO HAVE A VAGUE RECOLLECTION OF MEETING HIM ONCE BEFORE.

GOOD EVENING, SHOPKEEP. I REQUIRE ALL OF YOUR SHREDDED COCONUT.

NOTE THIS MAN'S INGENUITY! THIS IS THE KIND OF CREATIVITY THAT SHOULD INSPIRE ALL OF OUR BURNS INDUSTRIES EMPLOYEES!

EXCUSE MY IMPERTINENCE SIR, BUT HE'S ASKING PEOPLE TO BUY SMOKED AND CURED JIM CARREYS.

CELEBRITY JERKY FIGURINES
COLLECT THEM ALL!
AVAILABLE IN
RKEY or MEATLESS

HE'S A CORPORATE GENIUS, SMITHERS! THE KIND OF LEADER THAT I'M LOOKING FOR IN KWIK-E-MART UPPER MANAGEMENT. BRING THAT MAN TO ME IMMEDIATELY!

...AND CALL 911. I THINK I SHATTERED MY HAND.

THUD!

75

76

REMEMBER APU, *GREED* ISN'T AN *OPTION* FOR THE MODERN BUSINESSMAN--IT'S A *NECESSITY!* YOU HAVE TO CONVINCE YOURSELF THAT YOU DESERVE THE BEST! FROM NOW ON YOU'LL WEAR ONLY *ITALIAN SUITS!*

I HAVE ALWAYS FELT THAT I AM DESERVING OF THE BEST.

BUT UNTIL NOW, THE BEST CONSISTED OF *PROCESSED CHEESE* AND *SYNTHETIC FIBER BLENDS.*

HOW DO YOU LIKE YOUR LOBSTER THERMADORE?

IT IS MOST *APPETIZING!* AND NEVER HAVE I ENJOYED MELTED BUTTER IN SUCH *LARGE QUANTITY.*

S.S. WRITE-OFF

JUST STICK WITH ME MY HINDU FRIEND, AND *TOGETHER* WE'LL BUILD A KWIK-E-EMPIRE!

EXCELLENT!

EXCELLENT, *INDEED!*

LATER...

THANK YOU, LIMO DRIVER! I FOUND MY *COMPLIMENTARY BEVERAGE* MOST REFRESHING!

GOOD EVENING, UNCLE APU.

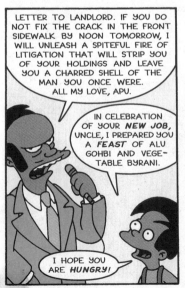

LETTER TO LANDLORD. IF YOU DO NOT FIX THE CRACK IN THE FRONT SIDEWALK BY NOON TOMORROW, I WILL UNLEASH A SPITEFUL FIRE OF LITIGATION THAT WILL STRIP YOU OF YOUR HOLDINGS AND LEAVE YOU A CHARRED SHELL OF THE MAN YOU ONCE WERE. ALL MY LOVE, APU.

IN CELEBRATION OF YOUR *NEW JOB,* UNCLE, I PREPARED YOU A *FEAST* OF ALU GOHBI AND VEGE-TABLE BYRANI.

I HOPE YOU ARE *HUNGRY!*

:YAWN:...I AM TOO TIRED TO EAT, JAMSHED. BESIDES, I ALREADY ATE WITH MY *NEW EMPLOYER.* ACCORDING TO HIM, I SHOULD ONLY CONSUME *POWER FOODS* SUCH AS RAW BLUEFIN TUNA, CAVIAR, AND FREE-RANGE GAMECOCK! A *SMART* BOY LIKE YOU SHOULDN'T WASTE YOUR TIME MAKING SILLY DINNERS!

BUT UNCLE, I--

GO NOW AND STUDY THE DEPRECIATION OF THE JAPANESE YEN!

GOODNIGHT, NEPHEW! MAY ALL OF YOUR DREAMS BE *FINANCIALLY SECURE.*

HI THERE, FOLKS! I'M TROY MCCLURE. YOU MAY REMEMBER ME FROM SUCH GRAND OPENINGS AS 'CHUCK WAGON, CHUCK WAGON, A GRAND DAY IS HERE' AND 'SPRINGFIELDERS REJOICE--FOR AT LAST YOU HAVE SHOETOWN.'

PLEASE, LOYAL CUSTOMERS, REMAIN CALM! THERE IS PLENTY OF APU AND QUALITY MERCHANDISE TO GO AROUND!

APU!

APU!

WHAT DO YOU MEAN THERE AREN'T ANY FREE PASSES UNDER THE NAME "SIMPSON?!"

YOU HEARD ME, LARD RUMP! THE COMPUTER SAYS YOU WERE THE GUY WHO ATE ALL THE PORK SQUEEZINS' AT THE KRUSTYLAND GRAND OPENING!

MK SUPER STORE

COLLECT YOUR PERSONABLES AND LEAVE THE PREMISES!

BUT WHY?

YOU ARE FIRED! THE SIMPSONS ARE HONORED GUESTS!

TICKETS

THANKS, APU!

NO, THANK YOU, LOYAL CUSTOMER. WE'RE COUNTING ON YOUR INSPIRING APPETITE FOR SALTED AND SUGARED FOODS TO SEE US THROUGH TO THE FIRST QUARTER EARNINGS!

TESTING...TESTING. ЗAHEM!...CAN I HAVE YOUR ATTENTION PLEASE?

WITHOUT FURTHER ADO, IT IS MY PLEASURE TO PRESENT TO THE PEOPLE OF SPRINGFIELD...

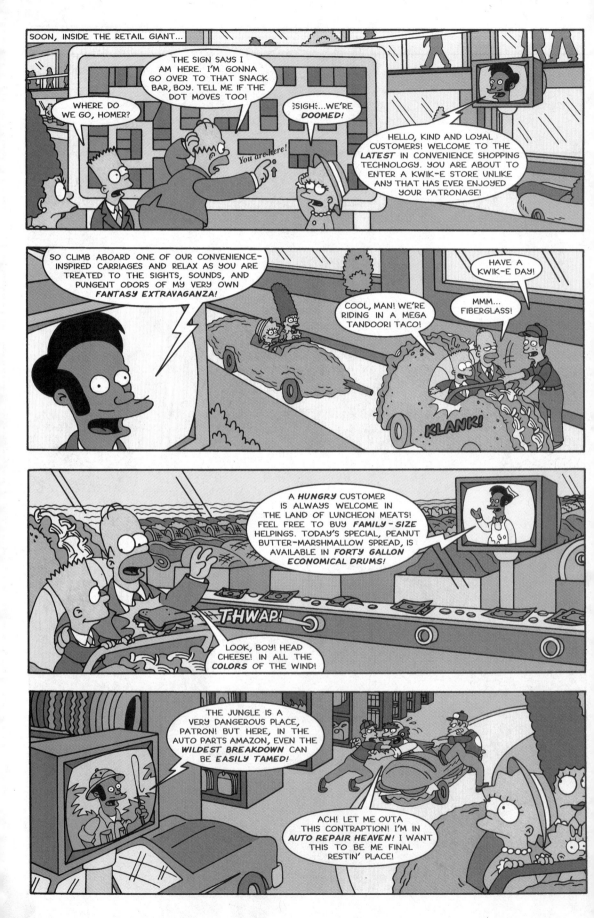

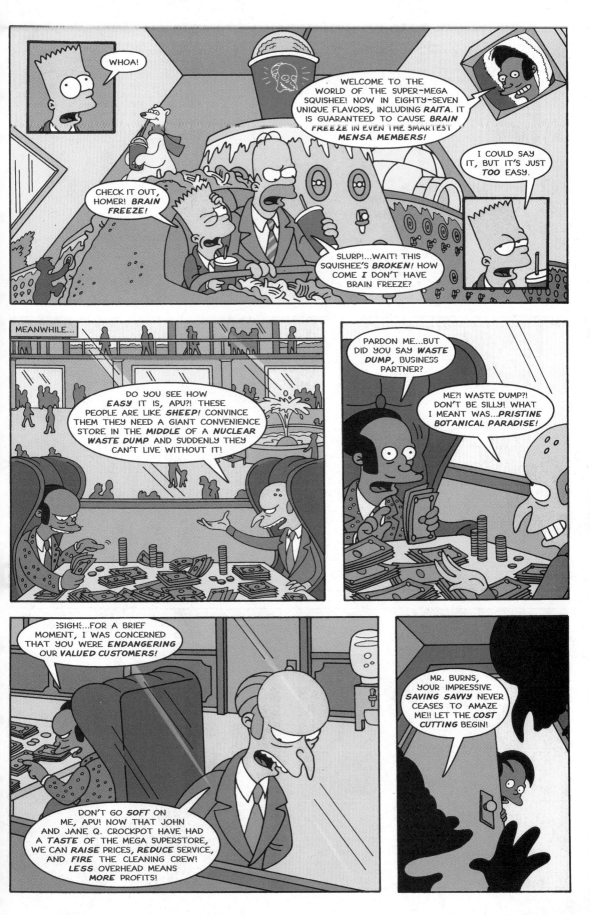

LATER...

WHAT ARE YOU DOING, UNCLE?

THANKS TO THE HANDS OF THIS GIFTED ESTHETICIAN, MY SKIN IS CLEAN AND REFRESHED!

SEE FOR YOURSELF!

I HAVE GOOD NEWS! THE CITIZENS OF SPRINGFIELD HAVE DECIDED TO HONOR YOU WITH A SPECIAL STATUE. YOUR PRESENCE HAS BEEN *REQUESTED* IMMEDIATELY!

:SIGH:...NOW THAT I HAVE DONE SO MUCH FOR THEM, IT IS CERTAINLY UNDERSTANDABLE!

PERHAPS IT WILL TAKE THE PLACE OF THAT CORRODING *MR. JEBEDIAH* STATUE.

KA-BOOM!

LATER...

WHY DID YOU BRING ME *HERE*, JAMSHED? I HAVE NO INTEREST IN REVISITING MY *IMPOVERISHED, BLUE COLLAR* PAST!

THIS IS WHERE *YOUR* MONUMENT IS LOCATED, UNCLE. ARE YOU READY FOR THE UNVEILING?

THAT IS MY *WORTHLESS* UNDER-THE-COUNTER HOODLUM BAT, JAMSHED! WHAT IS THE *MEANING* OF THIS?!

DON'T YOU SEE, UNCLE? IT *REPRESENTS* EVERYTHING YOU ONCE WERE TO YOUR APPRECIATIVE AND LOYAL CUSTOMERS! YOU WERE THERE TO *FIGHT* FOR THEM WHEN THEY NEEDED YOU!

I WAS THERE TO *WHACK* THEM IF THEY *STOLE* FROM ME! WHY WOULD ANYONE THANK ME FOR THAT?!

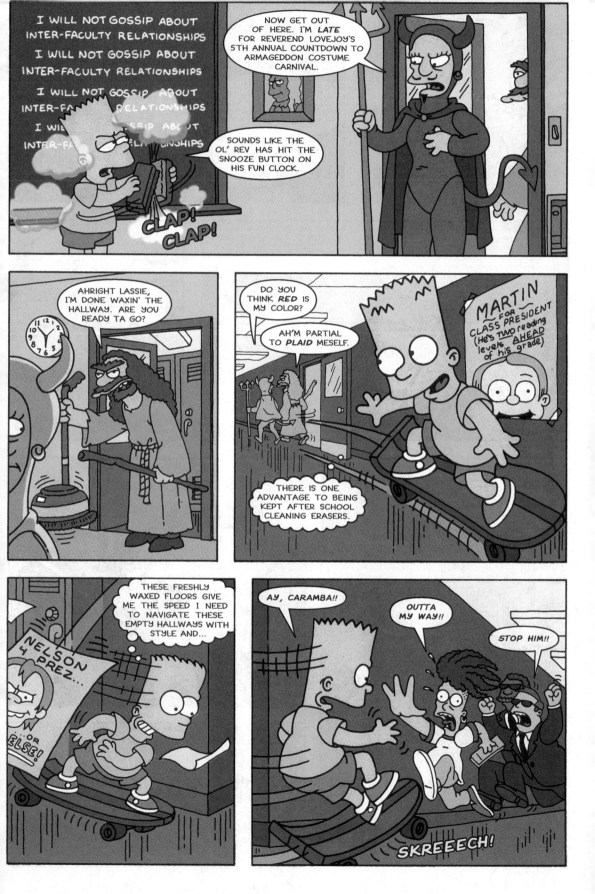

YOU MUST, OF COURSE, FIRST PURCHASE THIS OVER-ORDERED YET UNDER-SOLD ISSUE OF RADIOACTIVE MAN IN WHICH THE HERO EXPLAINS THE BENEFITS OF VOTING YES ON PROPOSITION 24 -- THE PROPOSITION WHICH WOULD CLOSE AMERICA'S BORDERS TO ALL IMMIGRANTS.

THIS SOUNDS LIKE A SHAMELESS WAY TO TRY AND BEEF-UP THE SLUGGISH SALES OF A POORLY CONCEIVED, THREADBARE PACKAGE OF RIGHT-WING PROPAGANDA.

RADIOACTIVE MAN
THIS BORDER CLOSED
PROP. 24

YOU ARE DANGEROUSLY CLOSE TO CROSSING A LINE THAT OTHERS BEFORE HAVE REGRETTED CROSSING. THE BOTTOM LINE, GENTLEMEN, IS NO *PURCHASE*, NO *FREE* I.D. CARD.

BANNED FOR LIFE

BUY NOW OR YOU'LL IT FOR THE REST OF YOUR LIFE!

HE'LL TAKE ONE!

BUT, BART, I DON'T REALLY WANT--

TRUST ME, PAL. IT'S ALL PART OF THE *PLAN*.

IN A MOMENT...

THERE YOU ARE. I HAVE DONE YOU THE SERVICE OF LAMINATING YOUR ID FREE OF CHARGE, MR. LATREC.

AW, *COOL!*

IF KRUSTY FALLS FOR YOUR ID, BY THIS TIME TOMORROW WE'LL BE ON A *CONCORDE TO EUROPE*.

RADIOACTIVE MAN

AT THE VERY LEAST WE CAN GET IN TO SEE MCBAIN'S LATEST R-RATED FEATURE, "THE WINTER OF MY DISMEMBERMENT," WITHOUT A PARENT OR GUARDIAN.

SUPERIOR SQUAD
NAME - Lou La Trec
AGE - 35
ALIAS - Eagle Eye

THE NEXT MORNING...

REMIND ME *WHY* I'M NOT TELLING MOM AND DAD THAT YOU ARE HEADING TO FRANCE WITH AN *IMPROPER CHAPERONE.*

BECAUSE I PROMISED TO BRING YOU BACK A SIZE "0" EVENING GOWN FROM CLAUDIE PIERLOT, MAKER OF FASHIONS WHICH ARE STUNNINGLY SIMPLE.

ᴇSIGH᷅...OH, RIGHT. SOMETHING THAT A YOUNG FRENCHWOMAN MIGHT WEAR WHILE ACCOMPANYING HER STRUGGLING ARTIST BOYFRIEND ALONG THE BANKS OF THE SEINE OR OUT TO THE THEATRE DES CHAMPS-ELYSEES TO SEE A SCANDALOUS PERFORMANCE OF STRAVINSKY'S "LE SACRE DU PRINTEMPS." AH, TO BE IN LOVE IN PARIS.

THAT'S A LOT TO ASK FROM ONE DRESS, LIS. AH, HERE COMES THE INTERNATIONAL AMBASSADOR OF AMUSEMENT NOW.

OH BROTHER, KIDS! EVERYDAY IT'S, KIDS, KIDS, KIDS. JUST ONCE I'D LIKE TO HAVE A CONTEST THAT ONLY LEGGY BLONDES CAN ENTER.

NOW, YOU BOYS HAVE A *SAFE* TRIP, *BEHAVE* YOURSELVES AND *ENJOY* THE FINE ART AND EXQUISITE CUISINE.

YEAH BOY, WHEN YOU GET HOME YOU CAN TELL ME ALL ABOUT WHAT IT'S LIKE TO EAT *REAL* FRENCH DELICACIES. MMM...FRENCH FRIES...FRENCH TOAST...FRENCH CUT GREEN BEANS!

I CAN'T *BELIEVE* YOU *FORGOT* THE BEARD! WE'RE SUNK.

YOU LOOK A *LOT YOUNGER* WITHOUT THE BEARD, LOU. YOU'RE LUCKY ALL YOU'VE GOTTA DO IS SHAVE-- I'VE GOTTA PAY SOME BEVERLY HILLS PLASTIC SURGEON A YEAR'S WORTH OF PRODUCT ENDORSEMENT MONEY TO KEEP MY BOYISH GOOD LOOKS.

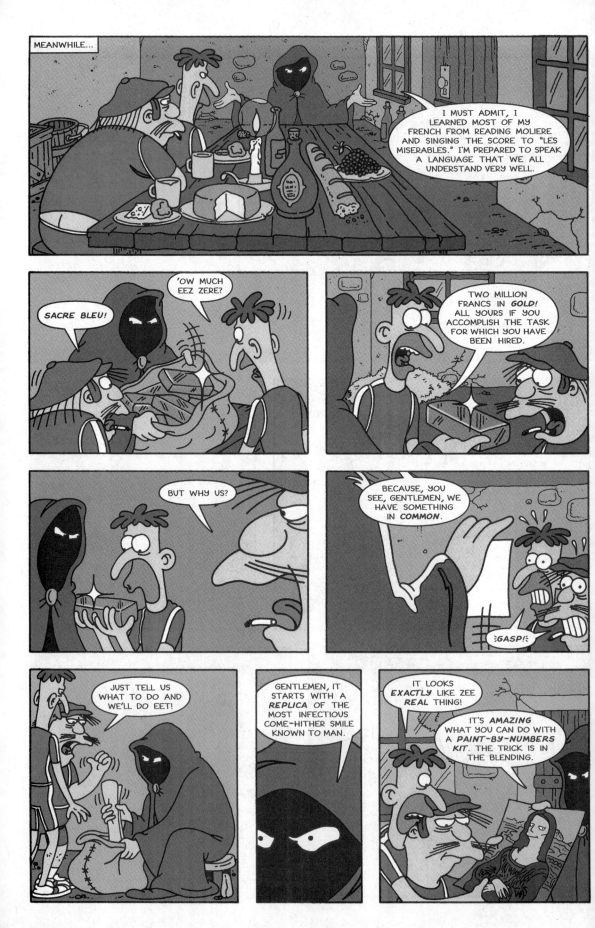

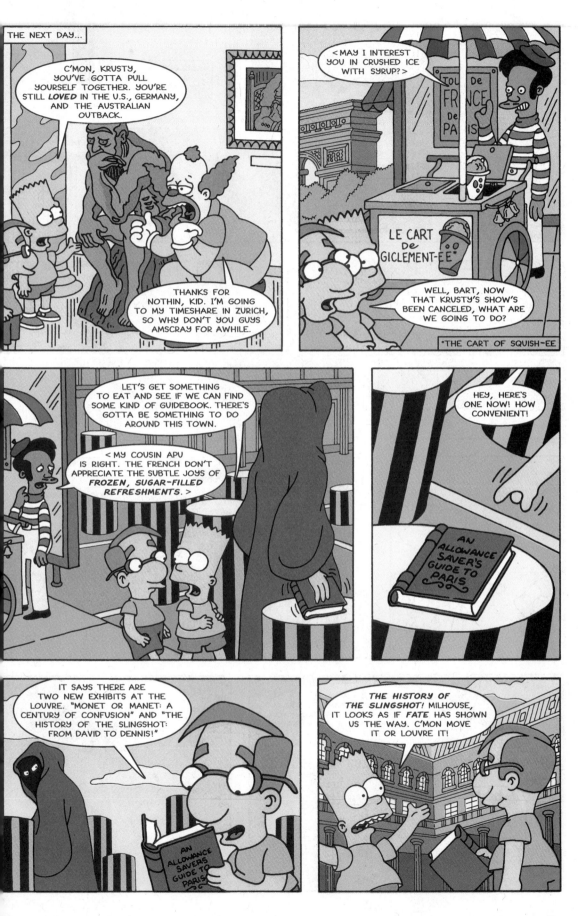

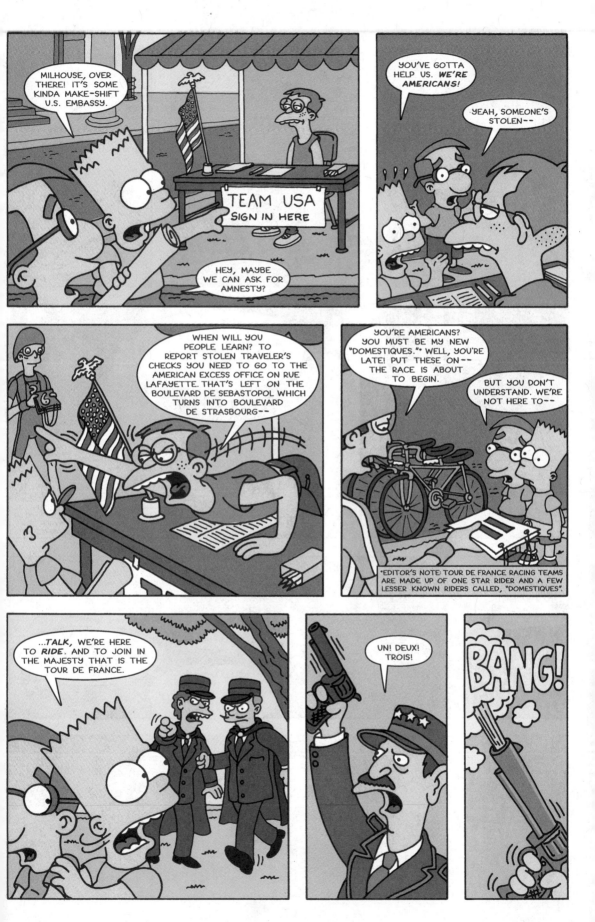

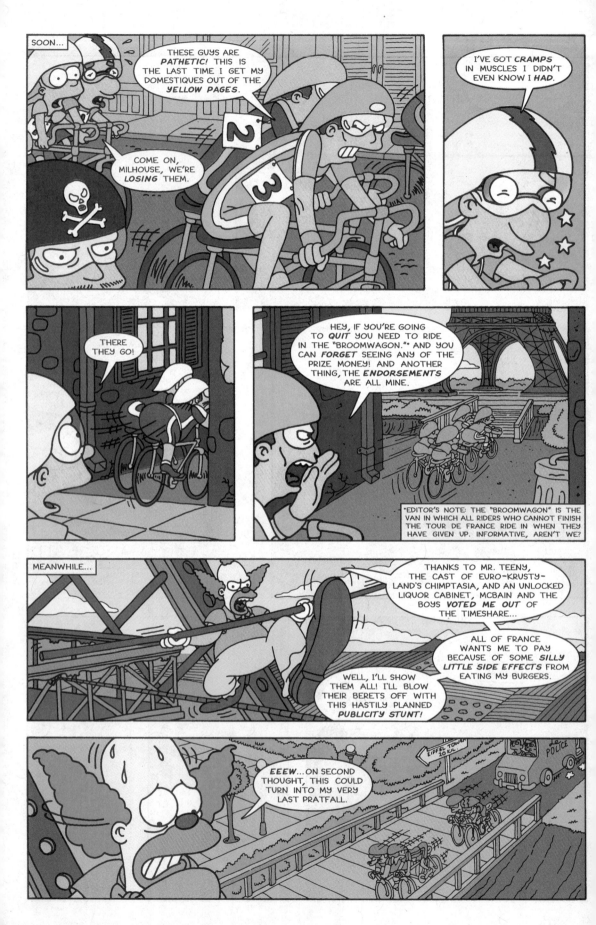

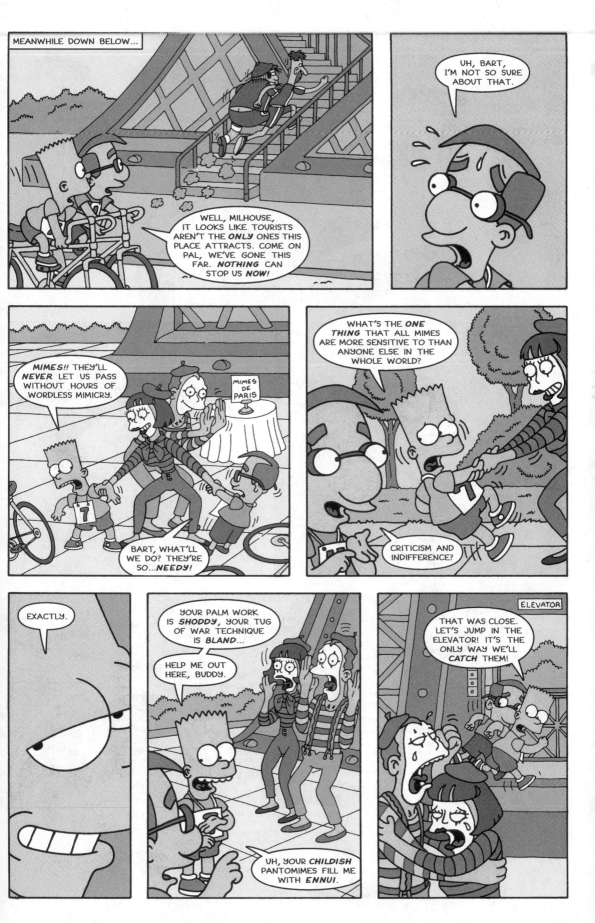

115

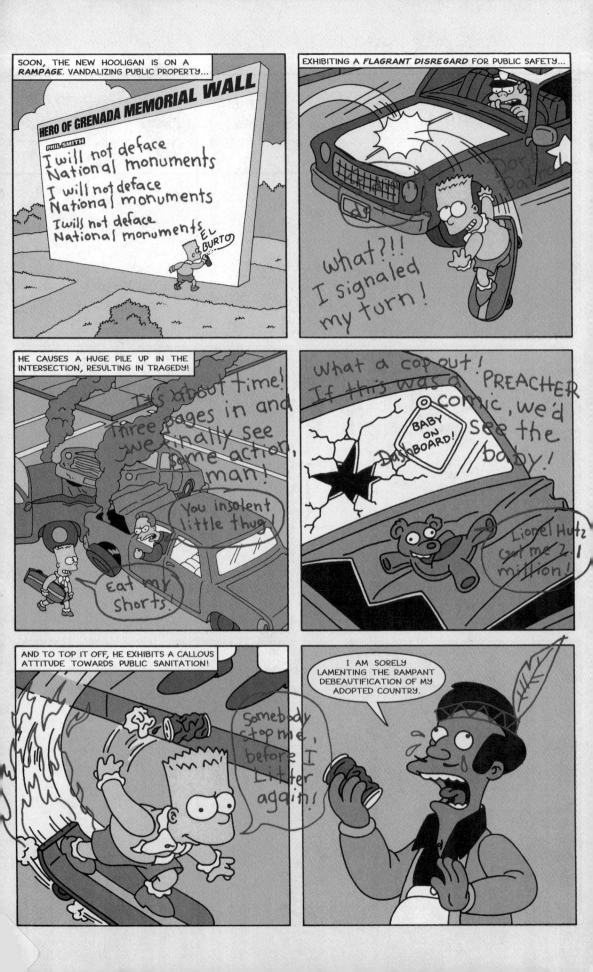

ONCE A MODEL CITIZEN, THE HOOLIGAN FINALLY GOES UTTERLY *STARK RAVING MAD*...

SPARE CHANGE... SPARE CHANGE... MUST... MAKE... PRANK CALLS! MUST BUY... SPRAY PAINT!

Must stop reading... Paranoid Propaganda!

JOE'S

MY GOODNESS! IT'S SO DISHEARTENING TO SEE SUCH WASTED POTENTIAL.

Thank you Mr. Boilermaker!

NOTHING IS SACRED...

practice random violence and senseless acts of mayhem!

GOOD LORD! ≷CHOKE!≷

IT CAN'T *BE!*

HE'S HOLDING KLUTZY THE KLOWN'S *SEVERED HEAD!!!*

As seen in John the Baptist Comics # 832 -- Rousin' Rev.

AND THERE'S ONLY *ONE WAY* IT CAN END...

PLEASE GIVE YOURSELF UP, SON! FOR *MY* SAKE.

MADE IT, MA... TOP OF THE WORLD!

Is it me, or has this guy been watchin' too many gangster movies?

BAM!

THESE TRANQUILIZER DARTS'LL BRING HIM DOWN!

How "humane"! He'll fall to his death but he won't feel a thing.

SO LET THIS SERVE AS A *WARNING* TO YOU, KIDS... ALWAYS PRACTICE GOOD CITIZENSHIP, OR YOU JUST MIGHT SUFFER THE FATE OF *CITIZEN SHAME.*

Come back! Shame! come back!

FIN

SCRIPTURE MEMORIZER
REV. TIMOTHY LOVEJOY

STINKS & XOLORS
SEYMOUR SKINNER

BED WETTERS
TODD & ROD FLANDERS

BART IS SUPERVISOR
HELEN LOVEJOY

STREET LINGO CONSULTANT
NED FLANDERS
(NED'S DOWN WITH THE HOMIES)